T0196429

There's Healing in His Wings

Vanessa K. Robinson

WESTBOW°
PRESS
A DIVISION OF THOMAS NELSON
& ZONDERVAN

Scripture taken from the Holy Bible, NEW INTERNATIONAL VERSION®.
Copyright © 1973, 1978, 1984 by Biblica, Inc. All rights reserved worldwide.
Used by permission. NEW INTERNATIONAL VERSION® and NIV® are
registered trademarks of Biblica, Inc. Use of either trademark for the offering
of goods or services requires the prior written consent of Biblica US, Inc.

Scripture taken from the King James Version of the Bible.

WestBow Press books may be ordered through booksellers or by contacting:

WestBow Press
A Division of Thomas Nelson & Zondervan
1663 Liberty Drive
Bloomington, IN 47403
www.westbowpress.com
1 (866) 928-1240

Because of the dynamic nature of the Internet, any web addresses or
links contained in this book may have changed since publication and
may no longer be valid. The views expressed in this work are solely those
of the author and do not necessarily reflect the views of the publisher,
and the publisher hereby disclaims any responsibility for them.

Any people depicted in stock imagery provided by Thinkstock are
models, and such images are being used for illustrative purposes only.
Certain stock imagery © Thinkstock.

ISBN: 978-1-4908-6042-8 (sc)
ISBN: 978-1-4908-6043-5 (e)

Library of Congress Control Number: 2014920782

Printed in the United States of America.

WestBow Press rev. date: 12/4/2014

Acknowledgements

Doxology

Praise God from whom all blessings flow
Praise Him all creatures here below
Praise Him above ye heavenly host
Praise Father, Son, and Holy Ghost
Amen

To God Be The Glory.

Contents

There's Healing
In His Wings

"In the year that king Uzziah died I also saw
the Lord sitting upon a throne, high and
lifted up, and his train filled the temple."
Isaiah 6:1

As for me, in the year that my life became plagued by one
illness or condition after another in rapid succession, I too
saw the Lord. I sought God like never before concerning
my health issues as they seemed to appear out of nowhere
with little or no warning. It was then that I realized that in
order to lessen the amount of obscurity between God and
me; my Uzziah(s) must die.

I have learned that my Uzziah is anything that hinders my
relationship with the true and living God. My Uzziah of
unbelief, my Uzziah of doubt, my Uzziah of murmuring, my
self-righteousness, my pride, my Uzziah of people pleasing,
and my Uzziah of acceptance of the status quo. I had been

1

convinced that I have no value of my own therefore I could never make a difference in God's Kingdom. I was satisfied with being in the shadows, working behind the scenes to make others look good, nurturing a false sense that this was my lot in life. I truly believed that I am here to help others reach their potential while failing to realize that my life has purpose as well.

It took many years for me to come to the knowledge that Psalm 139:14 includes me. It states, "I will praise thee; for I am fearfully and wonderfully made: marvelous are thy works; and *that* my soul knoweth right well." (KJV) I am a designer's original. This past year so many things have happened in my life but through it all, God showed me little glimpses of Himself to keep me encouraged. I went through some hard times but God was right by my side.

We all have a desire to be used by God but we don't realize He is not enlisting advisors to tell Him what He should do. Nor can we hope to be placed on His distinguished Board of Directors. When we pray, "God use me", we are surrendering our will to His and we don't know how He will choose to use us. This is His opportunity to put our faith on trial. We serve an awesome God who has the ability to take something ordinary and make it extraordinary for His glory. Psalms 68:35 states it this way, "You are awesome, O God, in your sanctuary; the God of Israel gives power and strength to his people. Praise be to God!"

So many things are going on in our world today. The perilous times mentioned in the Word are beginning to manifest themselves at an alarming rate. The weather is doing things that no one in our generation has ever seen before, people place so little value on the life of another, and sickness has plagued our society like never before. But in the midst of it all, we have this hope in Jesus Christ: The Best Is Yet To Come. He's coming back.

I have asked myself in the past the question, "Am I living rapture ready?" The answer at the time was a resounding, "No." No doubt the answer may still be no. All I know for sure is that because of God's grace and His mercy, I am still here. It is not because of my righteousness because by God's standards my righteousness is as filthy rags. God gave me the title and some instructions concerning this book almost ten years ago but I had to wait on further instructions. Yet when He directed me to move forward with this book, I thought it was unrealistic. I thought this was the very worst time to write about healing. I asked Him, "How am I supposed to write about healing in the midst of my own afflictions?" He said as He has before, "So they will know." He reminded me that nothing we go through is ever wasted. I knew I would have to trust Him.

In Matthew 15, Jesus refers to healing as the children's bread. But you would not know it when you visit the hospitals. If the enemy had his way, the saints of God would be cheated out of a benefit that clearly belongs to us. Matthew 15:25-28 KJV states,

> [25] Then came she and worshipped him, saying, Lord, help me.
>
> [26] But he answered and said, It is not meet to take the children's bread, and cast it to dogs.
>
> [27] And she said, Truth, Lord: yet the dogs eat of the crumbs which fall from their masters' table.
>
> [28] Then Jesus answered and said unto her, O woman, great is thy faith: be it unto thee even as thou wilt. And her daughter was made whole from that very hour.

I began to realize that it is going to take real faith to get me through the days ahead. I also believe God's Word. James 2:18 KJV states, "Yea, a man may say, Thou hast faith, and I have works: shew me thy faith without thy works, and I will shew thee my faith by my works." Verse 20 sums it up by stating, "But wilt thou know, O vain man, that faith without works is dead?" Recently God has taken me through a series of books by Smith Wigglesworth. He started me out with books on faith, then on believing, with two books entitled, Only Believe. Now my faith must stand trial because my actions must match my confession. I can say I trust God and I have faith but when circumstances arise to test my faith, am I able to stand on God's Word? Will my actions indicate real worship in spirit and in truth?

I went back and read 1 Peter 4:12-13 KJV, "Beloved, think it not strange concerning the fiery trial as though something strange is happening to you: But rejoice, inasmuch as ye are partakers of Christ's sufferings; that when his glory shall be revealed, ye may be glad also with exceeding joy." Sometimes it is easy to lose sight of who God is and what He can do. That is why it is so important to surround yourself with people who can stand with you in your time of trouble. You need positive people who will speak life into your situation. The Word says that one can chase a thousand, but two can put ten thousand to flight. Matthew 18:19, 20 KJV states, "Again I say unto you, That if two of you shall agree on earth as touching any thing that they shall ask, it shall be done for them of my father which is in heaven. For where two or three are gathered together in my name, there am I in the midst of them."

I have to be honest, no matter how you protect yourself from negativity; the enemy has a way of penetrating your fortress with someone who will try to keep you discouraged. Someone who will cause unnecessary problems to distract you and cause you to waste precious time trying to extinguish little fires they take great joy in setting. We have to pray for them and forgive them so that we don't lose our healing. It's sad that this happens but all too often it does, even among those who profess Christ as their Lord and Savior.

I have two reasons for addressing healing, the first is in obedience to God and the second reason is because God healed me in 1986. I know first-hand about God's healing virtue because He healed me against all odds when I had gangrene in my stomach and the bacteria had circulated throughout my system. According to a song by Tye Tribett, Same God (If He Did It Before), He is the Same God and if He did it before He can and will do it again.

Even though I spent six weeks in the hospital and underwent two surgeries, I know that the doctor did not heal me, my mother, as fervently as she prayed and as tenaciously as she held on to her faith, did not heal me, and I certainly did not and could not heal me. God healed me. Malachi 4:2 KJV states it this way, "But unto you that fear my name shall the Sun of righteousness arise with healing in his wings; and ye shall go forth, and grow up as calves of the stall." The NIV says, "But for you who revere my name, the Sun of righteousness will rise with healing in its wings. And you will go out and leap like calves released from the stall."

I feel spirit-led to give details about the time that I was healed of gangrene. That was my most intense encounter with the healing power of God. In 1986, as a result of a surgical procedure, I developed gangrene in my stomach. I was in so much pain and I sought medical attention several times in a two to three day period. I received countless diagnoses and was given prescriptions but nothing seemed to give even the slightest relief. Then on July 4th at around 2:00AM, I was rushed to the hospital for what everyone thought would be my last time, and the last time they would see me alive.

When I got in my mother's car, I asked God to please meet us there and to have someone in place that was anointed to help me. I lost moments of time because I was going in and out of consciousness. I thought I heard at one point the doctor discussing a need to admit me for further tests. It turned out that he indeed made that suggestion and my mother consented.

Later that day after being admitted, my family members started arriving. Some were local and some were from out of town. I had a tube in my nose from a machine that was pumping some dark green matter from my stomach. There was also a huge machine in my room in order to keep the air fresh because I was deteriorating from the inside. After numerous tests, the doctor informed my mother that they could draw no conclusions and that he would need to do exploratory surgery. My family, especially my brothers had such mixed emotions concerning this. Some thought it was cancer and did not think it would be wise to operate. We had been told that when you open someone up who is battling cancer, the air causes the cancer to spread more rapidly. My mother said she would let me decide. I told her to let them operate because I didn't believe death would hurt as much as I was hurting at the time.

On the day of my surgery, the doctor advised my mother to take my personal belongings home. He told her that if I survived the operation, I would be in intensive care indefinitely. So after a day of surgery I was placed in intensive care. My mother's best friend had stayed with her all day. She came in to see me and she told me that I was going to have a rough night but I would not die but live to proclaim God's Word. That night my temperature spiked to 108 degrees. The doctor called my mother to inform her of my condition and to prepare her for the worst. He told her that I probably would not make it through the night and if I lived, I would be so severely brain damaged that I would be in a vegetative state for the rest of my life.

He then told her that to his surprise I gave him the correct telephone number when he asked. She told him that we had that same number for years. He told her that she didn't understand; even at 103 degrees I should not have known my name. I should have been delirious. That fueled her faith and she began to pray. Two hours later, she stopped praying, my fever broke, and the person in the room next to mine died.

I always felt that my mother had dispatched my guardian angel to stand at my door to keep death at bay until my change came. The next morning the staff was baffled. They had to find me a room. I became known throughout the hospital as a living miracle and people came from all over the facility to see me. What people did not know is that my mother's best friend Ms. Odie Peterson, who stayed with my mother that whole day, spoke life over me. She had also told me that I was going to live to be a testimony of God's healing power. She said that I would have to tell my testimony wherever I go, as the Spirit leads.

So much has happened to me along life's journey. Bishop TD Jakes said it is a complement to our character when God trusts us with a trial. I began to visualize Job, when God asked the devil, "Have you considered my servant Job?" I envisioned in my mind, God asking satan, "Have you considered my daughter, Vanessa?" When I put it in that perspective, I can see my faith standing trial and God delivering me through every problem.

Michael Fackwell made the following observation and my niece included it on the cover of her booklet, *Voices: Real People Real Testimonies*. Fackwell stated, "The more Christians that come forward and talk about how God has intervened in their life, the more people will begin to realize that God is real, miracles do happen, and prayer works. This will inspire others to seek God and turn from their sins so that they too can know the peace and satisfaction that comes to a person who truly gives their life over to God."

I almost lost sight of that testimony and almost did not include the details in this book. Then one Sunday I was watching *The Potter's Touch*, a T. D. Jakes Ministry, when the guest evangelist gave the title of his message, it was entitled, *Dust Off Your Testimony*. Later, the confirmation came through loud and clear. I am so glad that Malachi 4:2 KJV reminded me, "But unto you that fear my name shall the Sun of righteousness arise with healing in his wings; and ye shall go forth, and grow up as calves of the stall."

Chosen In The Furnace Of Affliction

One morning after being released from the hospital, I awakened early because there was a sense that God had something to say to me. As I lay in bed I quietly listened as I asked Him to, "Speak Lord." He sent me to Isaiah 48:10, "Behold, I have refined thee, but not with silver; I have chosen thee in the furnace of affliction." I began to meditate on that Word and later I began to cross-reference it and read commentaries concerning this scripture trying to thoroughly understand what God was saying to me. Job 23:10 states, "But he knoweth the way that I take: when he hath tried me, I shall come forth as gold." My search for answers also led to a confirmation of 1 Peter 4:12-13 concerning the fiery trial. I was immediately taken to 1 Peter 1:7, "That the trial of your faith, being much more precious than of gold that perisheth, though it be tried with fire, might be found unto praise and honour and glory at the appearing of Jesus Christ."

My journey started when I noticed swelling in my left ankle that later progressed to my leg. Upon the advice of friends, I agreed to seek medical attention. It was discovered that I had high blood pressure and as a result, I had fluid in my leg. I was given blood pressure medicine to relieve the fluid. This did not work and the leg continued to get worse. I went back a second time and got the same diagnosis. I decided to go somewhere else and this time it was diagnosed as lymphedema. The foot and leg was so swollen that I could barely get around. Later, the foot gave way and I was walking on the side of it instead of the bottom. I tried hard to keep it straight but could not. The foot bones no longer supported the ankle bones causing them to jut toward the left side of my left foot while the foot, itself, looked as if it was dangling with my toes pointing to the right instead of straight ahead. My foot and ankle bones were terribly misaligned causing me to walk on my ankle instead of my foot.

I went to the doctor because I thought I had severely twisted my ankle. After several visits, they took x-rays but could not come to any conclusions. They sent me to get a CT scan and when they received the results, they called me to come in immediately. Blood was drawn and I was diagnosed as a diabetic. They gave me a prescription for an air cast. They had already prescribed crutches. The largest air cast they had would not fit because of the swelling and I was told that it would do more harm than good if I tried to wear it.

I began to feel so humiliated and seemingly thought of as absolutely nothing, and in some cases was treated that way. I had no insurance and no income and I was made to feel like because I lacked these things, my health and well-being was not important. Although I am a certified teacher, my inability to work because of my medical conditions changed the entire game plan for me. I had heard horror stories and now, I was the main character in one.

Some days when I returned from doctor visits I would feel so violated, like I had been stripped naked and paraded before the medical staff and the other patients. I have been asked by someone outside of the medical field if I was depressed. I told them that it is only by the grace of God that I was not. God kept me. After an appointment, I would just come home and pray in order to build myself up for the next appointment. I would have nightmares prior to some appointments which would elevate my blood pressure and glucose level.

One Saturday afternoon I fell asleep on the couch and when I awakened, my left foot and leg was swollen larger than I had ever seen them before. I was frightened and called a friend for prayer. She said she would come over and asked if her daughter could come. I welcomed it because her daughter is a nurse. Her daughter checked my leg out thoroughly and advised her mother to take me to the hospital and to make sure they keep me there. We arrived around 9:30PM and I was admitted to the hospital around 4:00AM. Two of my best friends stayed with me to make sure I was okay. One of them had to go home but the other one stayed until I was in a room. She stayed knowing she had to preach in a few hours.

The foot and ankle specialist came in the next day and ordered x-rays. He diagnosed my condition as Charcot joint caused by neuropathy, or nerve damage from the diabetes. He advised me that I would have to wear a cast for nine months because there was bone damage and then I would need to wear a brace for the rest of my life after surgery. His plan was to do reconstructive surgery on my foot.

I am not going to try to convince anyone that I walked on water through that whole ordeal. I have felt myself going under on several occasions and like Peter I cried out to Jesus, "Lord help me!" When I was going to physical therapy, the therapist discovered that the air cast that replaced the regular cast that was put on during my hospital stay had torn my skin leaving what the doctor termed an ulcer. I was advised of the dangers of being a diabetic with an open wound on my ankle and how it could lead to amputation of the foot and leg. I acknowledged that I understood the seriousness of what was happening at that time.

The leg with the Charcot joint is also the leg with lymphedema so there was a lot of lymphatic fluid escaping through the wound which was hindering the healing process. However, I had resolved that regardless of what it looks like, I trust God. God will get the glory in all that I am going through.

As for the furnace, I remember the story of Shadrach, Meshach, and Abednego in Daniel 3:19-25:

> [19] Then was Nebuchadnezzar full of fury, and the form of his visage was changed against Shadrach, Meshach, and Abednego: therefore he spake, and commanded that they should heat the furnace one seven times more than it was wont to be heated.

> [20] And he commanded the most mighty men that were in his army to bind Shadrach, Meshach, and Abednego, and to cast them into the burning fiery furnace.

> [21] Then these men were bound in their coats, their hosen, and their hats, and their other garments, and were cast into the midst of the burning fiery furnace.

[22] Therefore because the king's commandment was urgent, and the furnace exceeding hot, the flames of the fire slew those men that took up Shadrach, Meshach, and Abednego.

[23] And these three men, Shadrach, Meshach, and Abednego, fell down bound into the midst of the burning fiery furnace.

[24] Then Nebuchadnezzar the king was astonished, and rose up in haste, and spake, and said unto his counsellors, Did not we cast three men bound into the midst of the fire? They answered and said unto the king, True, O king.

[25] He answered and said, Lo, I see four men loose, walking in the midst of the fire, and they have no hurt; and the form of the fourth is like the Son of God.

I have learned and believe it to hold true in my situation that Jesus will show up when we are in our furnace. Our trials serve to glorify God. It gives Him the opportunity to flex His muscles if we put our trust in Him.

My friend who now resides in South Carolina advised me to write while I am in my proverbial "prison". She reminded me that the Apostle Paul wrote much of the New Testament while in prison. I began to listen with my spiritual ears to see what God was saying to me in this hour. After waiting for quite a few days, I heard three words. They were, "Let God Arise." I began to put my mind to work thinking that God wanted me to discuss His power and might, His infinite wisdom, sovereignty, and majesty. I thought He wanted me to let the church know that He will no longer tolerate the blatant disrespect we have for Him. When I got through with "my" plan, He said, "No, I was talking to you. Let God Arise, Vanessa." I have had to endure some humiliating things lately, but nothing was more humbling than to have my Heavenly Father address me in that way. He let me see that I am guilty of leaving Him out of the equation. He pulled back the curtains so that I could see how easily pride can rise up.

I felt the need to call on my God with humility so I went to Psalm 61:1-4:

> ¹Hear my cry, O God; attend unto my prayer.

> ² From the end of the earth will I cry unto thee, when my heart is overwhelmed: lead me to the rock that is higher than I.

> ³ For thou hast been a shelter for me, and a strong tower from the enemy.

⁴ I will abide in thy tabernacle for ever: I will
trust in the covert of thy wings. Selah

I am determined to go through my furnace because my
testimony can help others go through theirs'. God sees the
end from the beginning and He knew our purpose before
we were created. Jeremiah 29:11 tells us, "For I know the
thoughts that I think toward you, saith the Lord, thoughts
of peace, and not of evil, to give you an expected end."

In Luke 3:16, "John answered, saying unto them all, I
indeed baptize you with water; but one mightier than I
cometh, the latchet of whose shoes I am not worthy to
unloose; he shall baptize you with the Holy Ghost and
with fire." I understand now what the Apostle John meant
when he said Jesus would baptize us with the Holy Ghost
and with fire. The fire he is talking about is the furnace.

Goliath Had A Brother

The Sun of Righteousness that Malachi 4:2 is talking about is Jesus. Jesus had all power given unto Him by our Heavenly Father. According to Isaiah 53:4-5, "He has borne our griefs, and carried our sorrows: yet we did esteem him stricken, smitten of God, and afflicted. But he was wounded for our transgressions, bruised for our iniquities: the chastisement of our peace was upon him; and with his stripes we are healed." Matthew 8:16-17 confirmed this Word by stating, "When the even was come, they brought unto him many that were possessed with devils: and he cast out the spirits with his word, and healed all that were sick: That it might be fulfilled which was spoken by Esaias the prophet, saying, Himself took our infirmities, and bare our sicknesses."

Matthew 9:35 states, "And Jesus went about all the cities and villages, teaching, and preaching, and healing every sickness and every disease among the people." The good news is; Jesus is still in the healing business. Hebrews 13:8 says, "Jesus Christ the same yesterday, and to-day, and forever."

19

The next step in my journey caught me by surprise. To the naked eye, I let my guard down and was blindsided. In reality, I was so focused on what I was going through that over a period of time I may have encountered a moment where I grew faint. The enemy saw this as his opportunity to attack. The Bible warns us in 1 Peter 5:8 KJV, "Be sober, be vigilant; because your adversary the devil, as a roaring lion, walketh about seeking whom he may devour."

In 2 Samuel 21:15-17, Ishbi-benob the giant nearly killed David during one of his battles with the Philistines near the end of his reign. David grew faint and Ishbi-benob thought this would be a good time to avenge his brother Goliath's death. However, Abishai killed the giant, saving David's life.

During my research, some theologians said that Ishbi-benob was Goliath's brother and some just said he was a giant. However, I based my knowledge on what God spoke to me. When I was trying to figure out what was happening to me, God said, "Goliath had a brother."

When I went to the hospital for the second time in a little more than two months, I did not know what the problem was, but it felt so familiar to me. I started experiencing excruciating stomach pain accompanied by nausea and vomiting. I tried to be strong but I knew whatever it was, its intention was to take me out. I realized I was having almost a parallel episode of the 1986 gangrene experience. The problem was with my stomach and as stated earlier, I was surprised by the vicious attack.

The similarities with the time I had gangrene were uncanny. I wanted to talk to somebody but I was not led to anyone in particular. So many things that happened when I had gangrene were happening all over again. I told God that nobody could possibly know what I was experiencing but Him. That was the exact moment that He said, Goliath had a brother. I immediately grabbed my laptop and keyed in Goliath and it took me to several references of scripture and I read down until I got to 2 Samuel 21:15-17:

> [15] Moreover the Philistines had yet war again with Israel; and David went down, and his servants with him, and fought against the Philistines: and David waxed faint.

> [16] And Ishbibenob, which was of the sons of the giant, the weight of whose spear weighed three hundred shekels of brass in weight, he being girded with a new sword, thought to have slain David.

> [17] But Abishai the son of Zeruiah succoured him, and smote the Philistine, and killed him. Then the men of David sware unto him,

saying, Thou shalt go no more out with us
to battle, that thou quench not the light of
Israel.

Goliath had a brother. When God led me to research
this, I shared my findings with some others. Some were
fascinated and were inspired to research it further. I knew
that I did not have gangrene again but it was a strong
resemblance to what I had experienced. Then I began to
look at the contrasts to the situation and sought God for
revelation. I did not have fever, had no surgery to remove
the obstruction in my bowels, I was hospitalized six days
instead of six weeks and I never lost consciousness.

Yeah, Goliath had a brother and that brother caused
excruciating pain accompanied by nausea and vomiting but
it was not Goliath. God triumphed over him and he was
never resurrected. So when your healing is fully manifested
and Goliath tries to return, tell him in the name of Jesus
that God destroyed him and He will not resurrect him.
Ishbibenob can be defeated. He comes along to cause fear
and distractions. Do not get discouraged. Just continue to
walk by faith, not by sight.

Hold On, Change Is Coming

Whether you are saved or unsaved, you can recognize the hand of God. Most of us know the statistics concerning the recovery rate for what we are experiencing and we know when man reaches the end of his knowledge, God steps in. I challenge you to tell somebody else how God moved in your life. God does not use His healing virtue as a bargaining chip. He does not say, "I will heal you, deliver you and make you whole if you will serve me." If so, He would have to tell those of us who already serve Him that He won't allow us to be sick. As a matter of record, I had no major illnesses until I got saved. I was saved when I had gangrene. We should use our testimonies to strengthen and encourage others who are going through. Luke 22:32 KJV states, "But I have prayed for thee, that thy faith fail not: and when thou are converted, strengthen thy brethren."

One version of the Bible used the word restored instead of converted while two other versions used the word recovered. Jesus prayed for Peter that he would remain strong in the midst of his trials. He prayed that his faith would not fail. That is how we can get God to move on our behalf. It is our faith that moves God, not our sense of urgency, not our pleading, or by our many tears. It is with our faith.

We must help one another during our times of trouble. The following verses are evidence of this.

Romans 15:1-3

> We that are strong ought to bear the infirmities of the weak, and not to please ourselves. Let every one of us please his neighbor for his good edification. For even Christ pleased not himself: but as it is written. The reproaches of them that reproached thee fell on me.

Galatians 6:2

> Bear ye one another's burdens, and so fulfill the law of Christ.

As I researched these two passages of scripture listed above I discovered that the word bear has two different meanings. The first one, *anechomai*, means to sustain, bear or hold up against a thing. For example, most gardeners have to stake their tomato plants to support them and protect them because of the tomatoes they produce. The strength of the stake is transferred to the tomato plant and bears it up. When the Lord commands us to bear with one another in Colossians 3:13 and Ephesians 4:2, He is simply saying, "Put up with one another." We are to come alongside a weak (or sick) brother or sister and say, "Go ahead, lean on me. As long as I can stand, you will."

The second word is *bastazo* meaning "to bear, lift or carry" something with the idea being to carry it away or remove it. This proves that Christ's intercession for us was not a prayer He prayed, but a work He did. It was a work of going between to reconcile us to the Father and break satan's dominion. That is the work we must do as intercessors.

When I look at our young people in the school systems today, I am amazed that some of them have so many defenses built up at such an early age. I find myself asking the Lord, "How can we reach them?" Sometimes I ask, "Lord, can we reach them?" The world has glamorized sin through the media and our children seem to see the world offering them a way to make up their losses for the circumstances they have had to face in life. They are blind to the snares the enemy has set for them. As Christians, we must return to soul winning. We must bear the infirmities of the weak and we can do that by praying for them, fervently.

When Christ said on the cross, "It is finished", He was talking about His part. Now we must do our part. Paul wrote in Colossians 1:24KJV, "Who now rejoice in my sufferings for you, and fill up that which is behind of the afflictions of Christ in my flesh for his body's sake, which is the church:" Another translation says it this way, "Now I rejoice in my sufferings for your sake and in my flesh I do my share on behalf of His Body (which is the church) in filling up that which is lacking in Christ's afflictions." What could possibly be lacking in Christ's afflictions—our part. The Amplified Bible actually adds those words. "And in my own person I am making up whatever is still lacking and remains to be completed (on our part) of Christ's afflictions, for the sake of His body, which is the church."

What is lacking is the mediating, the going between, the distributing, and the enforcing. That's our part. I have often witnessed how we have become dispatchers in our prayers petitioning God to go by the hospitals and stop by the nursing home and visit the prisons. That's our part.

My research source instructed me that in Jeremiah 8:22, He is the balm of Gilead, but we must apply it. In Jeremiah 2:13 and again in Jeremiah 17:13, He is the fountain of life but we are dispensers of His living water. In Psalm 23:4, His is the comforting shepherd's staff, but He allows us the privilege of extending it. Not only did Christ bear our weaknesses, but He is continuously "touched with the feelings of our infirmities", as stated in Hebrews 4:15. He wants to touch us with the same compassion that we, too, might be bearers.

Just think about it, the Great Healer healing through us, the Great Lover, loving through us. Hebrews 12:24 reminds us that Christ established the new covenant with His blood but in reference to our part, 2 Corinthians 3:6 says He has made us able ministers of the new testament or covenant. As able ministers we are to administer something. What do we administer—the blessings and provisions of the new covenant. We are made able distributors of what Christ has already accomplished.

Again I admonish you to be encouraged. God's Word according to Habakkuk 2:3 says, "For the vision is yet for an appointed time, but at the end it shall speak, and not lie, though it tarry, wait for it: because it will surely come, it will not tarry." We must trust God to do His part. Our part is to draw on our believing faith with high expectations that our Lord and Savior will heal, deliver and restore us. We must develop a deep relationship with our Heavenly Father and His Son, Jesus. It's okay to have someone interceding for us, but we must learn to talk to God for ourselves so that we can pray others through during their time of trouble. When God entrusts you with

His gift of restored health, He has invested in your future. The ultimate act of gratitude would be for us to serve (worship) Him in spirit and in truth. That would be a good return on His investment.

God's Love Lifted Me

After six days in the hospital, I returned home with even more things that needed my immediate attention. I had a post hospitalization follow-up visit with my primary care physician. I had been feeling really lousy and when I went to my appointment, my blood pressure was low and my temperature was high. It was determined that I had pneumonia and I was put on antibiotics. The doctor also lowered the dosage of my blood pressure medicine and asked me to return to have my pressure checked in a few days. I returned once and it was still too low.

Before I had a chance to go back again to have my pressure checked, I had begun having severe pain in my leg with the Charcot foot. I went to the doctor and because of the pain and the increase in drainage; I was sent to the emergency room and was later admitted to the hospital. I was in so much pain that before they put me in a room in the emergency room, they sent me to get an ultrasound to determine if I had a blood clot in my leg. When I came back, they had a room for me and I called First Lady

Peterson's cellphone to see if she could come down with me to see what they were saying about my condition.

I was so glad she came because when the doctor picked up my leg, I screamed in pain. She laid hands on me and started praying. She remained there until I got a diagnosis and the news that they were preparing to admit me to the hospital. They gave me morphine for the pain. First Lady told me to call her when I got in a room. I thanked her for being there for me and she left.

I found out really quickly that the morphine did not agree with me. I began having waves of pain in my stomach and I thought I was allergic to morphine. I let the nurse know and he asked when I had eaten. He said sometimes medicines will react on an empty stomach. I had not eaten well in about ten days. I just did not feel like it. That morning I had a few spoons of a fruit cup and nothing else. It was my intention to pick up something when I left the doctor's office.

I thanked God for allowing me to get to the hospital on my own. I thanked Him for First Lady being there because this was the first time I had gone alone. Usually, one or both of my best friends have taken me.

This was my third time in the hospital in four months. It just did not seem real. I had worked until school closed for the summer and was looking forward to having the summer off. My life seemed to spiral out of control in a few months' time. I had the presence of mind to continue to look to Jesus. I was not in control, but He was.

The ulcer on my foot had started healing. My niece Linda, who is a nurse, came from Raleigh regularly and checked on it. She is such a woman of God; full of faith, inspiration, and encouragement. We had great fellowship with each visit and I told her about this book. I had been working on it for a long time but found myself making changes as I received instructions from God. She helped revive my love for writing and told me that I need to tell my testimony to give hope to others.

Just as I was collecting my thoughts, I was hospitalized. For the first time, others were able to see the foot Linda and I had been nurturing for some time now. The foot was swollen, dangling, and turned inward with the toes pointing toward my right foot. It had no feeling due to neuropathy and the bones were nonexistent in the foot. The ankle bones had nothing to support them and they seemed to be coming through the side of my foot. I actually walked on my ankle bone for a while because, as stated earlier, my left foot had fallen over and I was walking on the side of it.

I believed with all of my heart that as bad as it was, God could fix it. Several people came and had prayer with me. I was so encouraged when I was able to wiggle the toes on that foot for the first time since the onset of my illness. The young man and his wife that prayed with me really prepared me for what was about to happen. I was so happy that they had stopped by. The chairman of the deacon board and his sister came and had prayer with me also. They all strengthened me for the decision I was about to make.

I had been given a time limit to make a decision on the amputation of my leg. When the doctor who had been working with me from the onset came in and said it could not be reconstructed and that the ankle bone will eventually come out of the side of my foot, I agreed to the amputation. I was so much at peace when I did. I found that the surgery would occur the next day and I had to hurry to notify family members and friends.

One of my best friends, Reverend Beatrice Battle, came up to spend the day with me on the day of my surgery. My nieces Linda and her younger sister Ameenah came up as well. Their sister Renee had responsibilities on her job but the moment she was available, she was there and so was my other best friend, Minister Priscilla Evans.

Linda and Ameenah kept Beatrice and me laughing. The three of them made me so at ease going into surgery. I don't remember being in the recovery room after surgery, I just remember waking up in my room and that Renee and Priscilla had arrived. I knew this was just the beginning of my new life and I thanked God that it had started out so beautifully.

A physical therapist came in the day after I underwent surgery and told me I had to get up and walk some. I was concerned because I did not know what was required of me but I had said I would do whatever they asked because I needed to feel secure when I returned home. I did as she instructed to the best of my ability and was later informed that I would be going to the Bryant T. Aldridge Rehabilitation Center on the Nash General Hospital campus the very next day. I started getting my things together and calling family and friends to let them know I would be relocating.

On the day that I was to be transported to rehab, my nieces Trishonda and Renee and my nephew Montrell came to visit. I told them that I was going to give one hundred percent in rehab and if I feel that I am not ready to be discharged when the time comes, they cannot say it was because I failed in any way. That was the beginning of a twenty three day journey that I will never forget. They really worked with me from intake to discharge. I was okay when I came home because the staff at BTAR made sure I executed each task correctly. They also conducted a home evaluation so that I would know what changes needed to take place before I could return home.

My family and friends came by or called on a regular basis. I felt so blessed that I did not think about the surgery I had just gone through. My great nieces, Ashley and Illyanna, were able to come and visit in my room without having to meet an age requirement. My sister Audrey and her daughters and their sons came from Maryland as well as my niece Irish, her daughter and granddaughter all came in from Virginia. I just kept thinking on the goodness of God and how He allowed my family and friends to rally around me when I needed them the most. My brother John and his daughter Angela and her aunt Margie, my God brother Louis, my sister Wilhemina, my niece Jasmine Green, Minister Elaine Swanson, Mary French and Ms. Manuela Faulkner, Ray and Bill Dixon, Mamie Jenkins, Mary Parker, and my original crew: Renee, Linda, Ameenah, Beatrice and Priscilla.

Once I returned home, so many more have visited and are continuing to call. I thank God for everything that anyone has done for me. I pray His blessings upon every one of them. It's by God's grace and because of His mercy that I am still alive and that so many people have shown me so much love. God's love truly lifted me. Thanks Cynthia and

Jessica Jones, Lebanon A.M.E., Pastor JoAnn Boyd, New St. Mary, Dr. Patricia Brewer, Abundant Love Christian Center, Pastor Sonya Williams, Martha Whittle, Robin Boddie-Haggins, Linda Wilkins, Barbara Parker, Phyllis Parker, Wendy Greene, Carla Huddler, Vivian Johnson, Mary Harvey, Shirley Neville, Cheryl O'Neal, my brothers Dewitt and Hanks and my nieces Trishonda and Latasha, nephews Ronnie and Cameron, niece Pam, my sisters Mildred and Barbara and my nephew Jeff for showing me God's love.

I owe a special thank you to Mother Marion Simon, Sister Dianne Sanders, Pastor Willie and First Lady Alice Peterson, Brother Hubert and Sister Dorothy Joyner, Deacon and Deaconess Norman and Mamie Solomon. I appreciate the thoughts, prayers, cards, and telephone calls from so many people that I can't list them all. God sees you and He will bless you for blessing me.

I know first-hand what it means to have a support system and how important it can be. Even though I have never been married and I have no children, I was not alone. I know that God was with me but my family and friends were such an intricate part of my healing process. The Love of God truly lifted me. This was an example of God loving me through others.

FAITH: Forsaking All I Trust Him

It has been a while since I was able to attend church services. My friends who live in West Virginia, Jonathan and Michelle Woodfork, told me that I can still stay connected through the T.D. Jakes Ministries. The Potter's House stream their Sunday morning services live. Every Sunday I tune in and get blessed.

I was trying to find a specific sermon by T.D. Jakes on the internet when I ran across a sermon from the Potter's House by Dr. Jasmin Sculark entitled, Giants Do Die. I was truly blessed by this sermon. Recently while tuned in to T.D. Jakes, Dr. Jazz, as she is known, was again the guest evangelist for the morning service at the Potters House. God used her to speak directly to my heart. I felt that He was not finished so I looked her up and found that her church, which was then, Shiloh Baptist Church in York, Pennsylvania, airs their sermons on the internet also. She is now at Jericho City of Praise in Landover, MD.

I was watching a service one Sunday when Dr. Jazz said at the end of her sermon entitled, I'm Crossing My Jordan, that FAITH means Forsaking All, I Trust Him. I was in awe because she had already preached my soul happy. I almost leaped out of my wheelchair on several occasions. Early in my Christian walk, I had heard that fear means false evidence appearing real, but this was the first time in my thirty two years of being saved that anyone gave, in my hearing, an acronym for faith.

It was very timely, especially since I believed my faith was on trial. I find it very challenging to trust the systems in the United States that are supposed to assist us in our time of need. I used to hear the statement when I was growing up that said, "We're not looking for a handout but a hand up." Regardless of our participation by paying into the social security and the social welfare systems, when we have a real need, none is extended. I was unable to get help with my medical bills until I had accumulated a bill close to the national debt. I am very appreciative for the assistance because I have one less thing to worry about. Everyone who knows what I have been going through are shocked that I have not, at this point, been approved for disability benefits to help me as we assess how much I will recover physically for the purpose of returning to the workforce.

The country that was so strong and that offered so much to immigrants is now one that some of us are almost ashamed of. We have shifted our attention away from what made this country so great to just refusing to do anything to help our country move forward. The government parties are so divided, not because of pressing issues but because of who the president is. We are losing ground fighting among ourselves and the enemies of our country are just waiting for us to fall. They don't have to fire one shot. We are killing our country and it doesn't seem to matter.

This country was founded with a strong belief in God. Our founding fathers could not have made it without having faith in God. We have become so relaxed that we think we have the power to do anything and there will be little or no consequences. We are ignoring the signs of the times. I have always heard that ignorance is bliss, this holds true to some of our leaders who believe they are right in their actions to hinder our country from moving forward.

Our country is greater than our sexual orientations and legalizing controlled substances. This is God's country and forsaking all, I trust Him. While we are concerned with who someone is sleeping with, guns are still being carried into the schools by our children and they are causing mass destruction in the sense that our children are afraid to go to school because they know little Johnny got really angry on the playground yesterday and threatened to do harm to someone.

When I was teaching, a student came to me and told me that another student had a gun. I notified the resource officer who came and searched him but found nothing. A few days later, one of my other students informed me that the young man had slipped the gun to him and he returned it when they got off the bus at home. He said he made his friend promise that he would never bring it again. That could have been disastrous at that small alternative school. I prayed every morning for the safety of our students and staff, and on my way home in the afternoons, I thanked God for keeping us safe another day.

Mark 11:22 says, "And Jesus answering saith unto them, Have faith in God." This was not just a suggestion, it was a command. Jesus knows what God requires of us. God wants us to be men and women of faith. According to Hebrews 11:6, "But without faith it is impossible to please him: for he that cometh to God must believe that he is, and that he is a rewarder of them that diligently seek him" I have to constantly remind myself in the hard times I am now facing that faith is what moves God. My faith is not in the government systems but my faith is in God.

I cannot assume that everyone knows what faith is, so I consulted the dictionary on the matter. According to the dictionary, faith is the confident belief or trust in the truth, value, or trustworthiness of a person, idea, or thing. Faith does not rest on logical proof or material evidence. As a theological virtue, faith is a secure belief in God and a trusting acceptance of His will. 2 Corinthians 5:7 states, (For we walk by faith, not by sight:)

In order to keep moving forward with all that I have been going through, I know I must trust God and have faith in Him. I once preached a sermon on faith entitled, Faith: From Desperate to Deliberate. I can assure you that this message helped prepare me for what I am now going through. I had to reassess who I am in Christ and what He means to me. I could not tell others, with strong conviction, the importance of having a relationship with the Lord without having one myself. Now that my faith is literally on trial, will my Defense Attorney (Jesus) have enough evidence to get a favorable ruling?

It is my faith in a loving Father that keeps my mind steadfast when I feel that people in positions to help do not seem to care. Psalm 27:13, 14 says, "I had fainted, unless I had believed to see the goodness of the LORD in the land of the living. Wait on the LORD: be of good courage, and he shall strengthen thine heart: wait, I say, on the LORD." The Word of God tells us that we can have faith that we will see His goodness while we are still living. Then it tells us to do what seems to be the hardest thing to ask a human being. It tells us to wait. Waiting is not always easy. We cannot blame Abraham and Sarah for trying to "help" God administer a promise. We, too, try to devise ways to "help" when we have to wait.

While we are waiting on God, we are not expected to just sit still day after day doing nothing. We who have problems being ambulatory can call others and give them words of encouragement, email people with words of faith, check on an elderly person and create a plan if they are in need of something that we cannot deliver. As I wait on God to move on my behalf, I am jotting down things or services that I can offer others. My desire is to visit the sick and share my testimony. I want people to know that there is hope and that God has the last say.

People find it so hard to believe that I am okay about having my leg amputated. They think I am in denial because I am not constantly upset about it. The way I figure it is, I have two choices, I can accept it and look for ways to move forward or I can sit around and worry my life away. People used to say that worrying was like rocking in a rocking chair, you do a lot of work but you don't get anywhere. I prefer expending my energy in a more focused and positive way. I want to be there for people who need to talk about their condition with someone who has been through some trials and tribulations. I want to extend the Shepherd's rod of comfort to someone who is going through something. As I stated earlier, I am so grateful for the people who offered their support when I was making my decision, having the surgery, and battling back through rehabilitation. I thank God it did not stop there. My niece Jasmine assisted her mother in setting my house up so that it was wheelchair

accessible before I came home. Most teenagers would have been ready to go shopping and enjoying life while home from college.

Forsaking all, I trust Him. He has been there with me and showing me glimpses of Himself to keep me encouraged. He is not a respecter of persons; He will do it for all who have faith in Him.

Psalm 130:5 states, "I wait for the Lord, my soul doth wait, and in his word do I hope." One thing we can certainly do while we wait is to search God's Word with the intention of standing steadfast and unmovable on His promises. Psalm 119:49 says, "Remember the word unto thy servant, upon which thou hast caused me to hope." In verse 81 of the same chapter, the author states, "My soul fainteth for thy salvation: but I hope in thy word." Even from my wheelchair, I ask God to order my steps in His Word according to Psalm 119:133.

In the furnace of my afflictions I can say with Jeremiah in Lamentations 3:21-23, "This I recall to my mind, therefore have I hope. It is of the LORD's mercies that we are not consumed, because his compassions fail not. They are new every morning: great is thy faithfulness." God is faithful. But how can I recall this in my mind? I can share my testimony and how it lines up with the Word of God. Forsaking All, I Trust Him.

There Is Hope

As you can see, my life took some unexpected turns in less than a year. I had no idea that my life would be so different in a matter of just a few months. I was diagnosed with high blood pressure due to a doctor visit for a severely swollen leg and ankle; it was shortly afterwards revealed that I had lymphedema. I think the thing that sticks in my mind the most is when my foot collapsed and I was walking on the side of it on my ankle bone. Only then was it diagnosed that I had diabetes with very severe neuropathy that had attacked and deteriorated the bones in my left foot. This condition was called Charcot joint. I was hospitalized on another occasion for severe stomach pain and diagnosed with an obstruction in my lower bowels and it was during that time that it was discovered that I have a large hernia that needs to be repaired.

In a matter of a few months and after a bout with pneumonia, I went from crutches and an air cast to four professionals agreeing that a below the knee amputation would be the best course of action for my left leg. I was scheduled for laser therapy on one eye and an injection in the other. I had to postpone dealing with my newly developed impaired eyesight in order to have the amputation. I know that it was God who orchestrated my path and made it possible for me to get back to the business of my eye appointments after the amputation. I was experiencing hemorrhaging from the vessels in the back of my eye that at one time actually obscured my vision. The blood that came up in my eye was so thick that it completely blocked my vision.

I have to be honest, it did cause me to fear and my mind raced because I have a love for reading as well as for writing. At that point, I could do neither.

I prayed because I knew that I was already limited in what I could do. I had only been home from the hospital and rehab about ten days. I was adjusting to life in a wheelchair and the thought of not being able to see was very frightening. God immediately quieted my spirit and the next day I called the doctor and they told me to come in immediately. I had to find transportation so I accepted a later appointment. My brother Hank came to my rescue. The doctor checked me out, advised me on what to do, and sent me on my way. I followed his advice and things seem to be going fine. My vision has not improved, but I have not experienced the bleeding like it was originally. I am not currently receiving laser therapy but I am now having injections in both eyes.

I am not trying to solicit your sympathy for what I have gone through nor for what I am still going through. I just want people to know that when your mind is free your body has no choice but to come under the subjection of God. There is hope. I know that as long as there is life, there is hope. When I think of what God told Paul when he asked that the thorn be removed from his side, I know it holds true for me as well. God's grace is sufficient.

Philippians 1:20 assures me I can boldly confess my healing. The verse says, "According to my earnest expectation and my hope, that in nothing I shall be ashamed, but that with boldness, as always, so now also Christ shall be magnified in my body, whether it be by life, or by death." When you are in Christ, death is not an ending, it is a beginning. Paul is telling us whichever way God chooses to heal us; it will be to the glory of Christ.

There is hope. Hope is future, faith is present. God's Word says in Jeremiah 29:11NIV, "For I know the plans I have for you," declares the LORD, "plans to prosper you and not to harm you, plans to give you hope and a future." I believe His Word, therefore I have hope. Even though I am going through a financial drought right now, I feel that it is more blessed to be penniless than to be hopeless.

When I have hope, I can believe God's Word to Moses in Exodus 3:14, "I AM THAT I AM. Tell them I AM hath sent you unto them." He did not say I WAS for those who may be regretting the past, nor did He say I WILL BE for those who fear the future. But for those that live in the moment, we can find Him here. He said my name is I AM. He is constantly with us, making provisions for the promise to give us hope and a future.

When we are seeking God concerning our health or anything else that concerns us, we must learn to seek Him with our whole heart. We know mentally that God is good and that He is worthy to be praised but we have a problem getting that message to resonate in our heart. I am not talking about the blood pumping organ in our chest; I am talking about the human spirit, the core or innermost part of our being. When we are born again it is the rebirth of the human spirit. Romans 10:10 states, "For with the heart man believeth unto righteousness; and with the mouth confession is made unto salvation."

I used to wonder how I could get the knowledge of God from my head to my heart. No one that I asked was able to tell me with any certainty. Most of them avoided the question altogether. Then, I asked the Holy Spirit to teach me, and He did. I began to read and study the Word. I did not have access to many resources back then. Today there are an abundance of resources that are available. Because I was on a quest to know Him, the few resources I found helped me tremendously.

People think that we can somehow use faith and hope to manipulate the hand of God. If we spend sufficient time reading and studying His Word we will see certain attributes of His character that will let us know that this is not the case. Psalm 37:4, which states, "Delight thyself also in the LORD, and he shall give you the desires of thine heart." Delight here means to make God the joy of your life, to rejoice in Him. When we form this relationship with God we will ask for nothing but the things that pleases Him. There are no magic tricks that will get us what we want from God and because of how this thing has been taught it causes some people to turn back from following God. Their faith was strong but they did not get what they had requested from God. Sometimes God's answered prayer may differ from what our expectations have been and we fail to recognize that God has answered our prayers.

To be perfectly honest, when I asked God to heal my leg I had no idea that the method He would employ would be amputation. But in making that decision He blessed me with a peace that was far beyond my understanding. There can't be any "Oops!" in amputations as if you can duct tape or crazy glue something back on. I had to know I was making the right decision. God's Word according to Romans 8:28, "And we know that all things work together for good to them that love God, to them who are the called according to his purpose." God is going to get the glory out of this.

God in His infinite wisdom sent His Son Jesus to help us in the Earth realm. Jesus was our provision for salvation. As an infant He caused a king great anxiety, as a child He amazed doctors and lawyers, and in manhood He walked on water, calmed a raging sea, preached the gospel to the poor, healed the broken hearted, preached deliverance to the captives, recovered sight to the blind, and set at liberty them that were bruised.

His earthly family had neither name, wealth, nor influence. He never wrote a book but all of the libraries in the United States could not hold all of the books written about Him. He has never written a song but He has provided the theme for more songs than all of the other themes combined.

The names of past influential people such as scientists, philosophers, and theologians have come and gone, but His name is above every name. He lives after more than a two thousand-year span from His crucifixion until this present generation. Herod could not kill Him, satan could not trick Him and death, hell and the grave could not hold Him. The good news is Jesus Christ is the same yesterday, today, and forever according to Hebrews 13:8.

The songwriter wrote, "My hope is built on nothing less than Jesus' blood and righteousness." Psalm 31:24 tells us, "Be of courage, and he shall strengthen your heart, all ye that hope in the Lord." Psalm 33:18 confirms Malachi 4:2.

It states, "Behold, the eye of the Lord is upon them that fear him, upon them that hope in his mercy."

There is hope. Romans 15:4 states, "For whatsoever things were written aforetime were written for our learning, that we through patience and comfort of the scriptures might have hope." Where does the Apostle Paul say we are to find comfort? He says it's in the scriptures and that the scriptures were written for our learning. We are responsible for building our relationship with God the Father, Jesus the Son and the Holy Spirit. We can do this by reading and studying the Word, attending worship services, Bible study, Sunday School, and engaging in both private and corporate prayer and devotions.

Healing

While in my furnace of affliction, I relied heavily upon God's Word. The scriptures have the power to comfort us through our trials and tribulations. Some people have marveled that I am not bitter about what I have been going through. I asked them would my bitterness change things for the better and their answer was no or I don't think so. I just want to move forward and God has given me the strength to do it. God has been my hope through everything I have had to face. Things were coming at me so quickly that if I would have dwelled on them instead of looking to God, I would not have made it this far.

My God is Awesome and He is bigger than any of the things that have happened to me. He kept showing up during my struggles. He assured me that the Sun of Righteousness would arise with healing in His wings almost ten years before the high blood pressure, lymphedema, diabetes, neuropathy, Charcot foot, bowel obstruction, hernia, impaired vision, and the amputation.

I thought He was instructing me so that I could be a source of comfort and encouragement for my best friend who had leukemia, but He knew that I would sometimes need to encourage myself in my time of need. I began to understand why He spoke those three words to my spirit. He simply said, "Let God Arise." I know now that He has to reign supreme in my life in order for me to remain steadfast and unmovable for such a time like this.

I had to ward off negativity because people wanted me to be bitter about who didn't come to see me or who didn't call to check on me. I told them that in all fairness to the ones who did come by and the ones who did call, I refuse to expend energy on that kind of thinking. I could not lose my focus on what was important. The people God placed in my life were a vital part of my healing process. I was so encouraged when my God brother, Louis Simon would accompany me to my therapy sessions. My niece Linda had accompanied me also. I told her that I felt like the Karate kid—wax off, wax on. But through it all, I challenged myself to succeed at all of the tasks I was assigned by the therapists. This whole experience has changed me in so many ways. Physically, I have one leg, have dropped a few pounds and my hair has gone through some changes due to strong medicines and the anesthesia, but the real changes are the ones no one can see—but God.

2 Chronicles 7:14 KJV states, "If my people, which are called by my name, shall humble themselves, and pray, and seek my face, and turn from their wicked ways; then will I hear from heaven, and will forgive their sin, and will heal their land." So now we know what we must do, in addition to having faith. We must humble ourselves, pray, seek God's face, and turn from our wicked ways. As Christians, we may already be doing these things but we need to turn it up a notch or two. The powers of darkness have intensified their attacks. We know that in the end we win, but we do not have to wear some of the battle scars that we might otherwise have.

As we grow in grace, the Word shows us God's will for us in 3 John 2 KJV, "Beloved, I wish above all things that thou mayest prosper and be in health, even as thy soul prospereth."

I have compiled a partial list of healing scriptures that will help us to understand what God's Word says about this gift. When visiting my friends in Virginia, we used to attend Jabbok Ministries in Forestville, MD. Their theme is NOFO-not one feeble one. They are referring to the millions of people who came out of Egypt with Moses. Can you imagine that many people and not one sick or weak person among them? Well, we serve the same God.

Read all of the verses in each section aloud or have someone read them to you. Romans 10:17 says, "So then faith cometh by hearing, and hearing by the word of God." This will allow them to get into your spirit. Just like the medications we are willing to take, the Word acts as medicine to those who believe.

Proverbs 12:18

> Reckless words pierce like a sword, but the tongue of the wise bring healing.

Proverbs 16:24

> Pleasant words are a honeycomb, sweet to the soul and healing to the bones.

Isaiah 58:8

> Then your light will break forth like the dawn, and your healing will quickly appear; then your righteousness [Or your righteous One] will go before you, and the glory of the LORD will be your rear guard.

Jeremiah 33:6

> "Nevertheless, I will bring health and healing to it; I will heal my people and will let them enjoy abundant peace and security.

Malachi 4:2

> But for you who revere my name, the Sun of righteousness will rise with healing in its wings. And you will go out and leap like calves released from the stall.

Matthew 4:23

> Jesus went throughout Galilee, teaching in their synagogues, preaching the good news of the kingdom, and healing every disease and sickness among the people.

Matthew 9:35

> Jesus went through all the towns and villages, teaching in their synagogues, preaching the good news of the kingdom and healing every disease and sickness.

Luke 6:19

> And the people all tried to touch him, because power was coming from him and healing them all.

I guess you ask, "How can we touch Him today?" Through prayer, faith in Him, spending time in the Word, and building a relationship with Him.

Luke 9:6

> So they set out and went from village to village, preaching the gospel and healing people everywhere.

Acts 3:16

> By faith in the name of Jesus, this man whom you see and know was made strong. It is Jesus' name and faith that comes through Him that has given this complete healing to him as you can see.

The above scripture starts by saying, by faith in the name of Jesus. That's powerful.

Healed

Because of my tests, I have a testimony. The Word of God declares in Revelation 12:11, "And they overcame him by the blood of the Lamb, and by the word of their testimony; and they loved not their lives unto the death." We can overcome satan because with our testimony, we can give others hope. I constantly say this and I will repeat it as many times as necessary because I believe it is true. The strongest weapon is satan's arsenal is discouragement. The enemy knows if he can steal your hope, he can kill your joy. That's why it is vital to know the Word. Jesus, when He was tempted by satan, used the Word as His weapon in Matthew 4: 4, 6, 7, 10.

In the midnight hour when people lie awake, the enemy creeps in and uses discouragement. He can be very convincing when it looks like the odds are stacked against you. I thank God that Ms. Odie Peterson prepared me for the midnight hour experience that she knew I was about to face when I had gangrene. It is my deepest desire to prepare others.

I can't emphasize enough the importance of a good support system. When I had gangrene I had my mother and Ms. Odie Peterson and now I have my family and friends. I want to make myself available to others as a source of support. Hold on to the promises of God. Confess them, meditate on them, and believe them, so that you will have an anchor in the midst of your storm.

These are some scriptures on healed, yes past tense because with His stripes we are healed.

Psalm 30:2

O LORD my God, I called to you for help and you healed me.

Psalm 107:20

He sent forth his word and healed them; he rescued them from the grave.

Isaiah 53:5 KJV

But he was wounded for our transgressions, he was bruised for our iniquities: the chastisement of our peace was upon him; and with his stripes we are healed.

Jeremiah 17:14

Heal me, O LORD, and I will be healed;
Save me and I will be saved, for you are the
one I praise.

Hosea 11:3

It was I who taught Ephraim to walk, taking
them by the arms; but they did not realize it
was I who healed them.

Matthew 4:24

News about him spread all over Syria, and
people brought him all who were ill with
various diseases, those suffering severe pain,
the demon possessed, those having seizures,
and the paralyzed, and he healed them all.

Matthew 8:8

The centurion replied, "Lord, I do not
deserve to have you come under my roof.
But just say the word, and my servant will
be healed."

Matthew 8:13

Then Jesus said to the centurion, "Go! It will
be done just as you believed it would." And
his servant was healed that very hour.

Matthew 9:21

> She said to herself, "If I only touch his cloak, I will be healed."

Matthew 9:22

> Jesus turned and saw her. "Take heart, daughter," he said, "your faith has healed you." And the woman was healed from that moment.

James 5:16 KJV

> Confess your faults one to another, and pray one for another, that ye may be healed. The effectual fervent prayer of a righteous man availeth much.

1 Peter 2:24 KJV

> Who his own self bare our sins in his own body on the tree that we, being dead to sins, should live unto righteousness: by whose stripes ye were healed.

It is time for us to walk in our God-given authority. God spoke the world into existence and we can use that same creative power backed by the promises in God's Word to speak our healing into existence. We should make it a habit of renouncing any negative things that are said about our circumstances because words have life. The Word says,

"Death and life are in the power of the tongue: and they that love it shall eat the fruit thereof." Proverbs 18:21

We cannot control what others say about our circumstances. They may even be courteous enough not to say what they are thinking in our presence. We should make it a habit when we pray to bind up any negative conversation concerning us and loosing healing and life.

I know this just seems to be so much to deal with for those who are literally fighting for their life. That's why a good support system is so necessary. Walk in authority even from your bed of affliction. Plead the blood of Jesus over your life and your health. Ask someone that you can depend on, to agree with you in prayer to break, crush, and destroy the strongholds that are erected by someone speaking negative things over your life.

We must bear the burdens of others. We must be vigilant in caring for the things of others that God may care for ours. That is His great command, that we love one another, as He has loved us. He died for us, are we willing to lay our lives down, in prayer, for a friend?

Strength

Romans 15:1 states, "We then that are strong ought to bear the infirmities of the weak, and not to please ourselves." When I read this I immediately visualized a support system. The second part of that verse reminds us that there should be no hidden agendas or motives in bearing the infirmities of others. We should do it because it is the Christian thing to do.

Proverbs 14:26 promises, "In the fear of the LORD is strong confidence: and his children shall have a place of refuge." Joel 3:10 tells us, "Beat your plowshares into swords and your pruning hooks into spears: let the weak say, I am strong." Spiritual warfare has intensified. There is no place in God's army for cowards. He admonishes us to say that we are strong even in our weakness, because we can have what we say. Then we can say like 2 Corinthians 12:10 KJV, "Therefore I take pleasure in infirmities, in reproaches, in necessities, in persecutions, in distresses for Christ's sake: for when I am weak, then am I strong."

We must be like Abraham. Romans 4:20 says, "He staggered not at the promise of God through unbelief; but was strong in faith, giving glory to God." "Finally, my brethren, be strong in the Lord, and in the power of his might." Ephesians 6:10

Exodus 15:2

> The LORD is my strength and my song; he has become my salvation. He is my God, and I will praise him, my father's God, and I will exalt him.

Numbers 14:17

> Now may the Lord's strength be displayed, just as you have declared.

Judges 15:19

> Then God opened up the hollow place in Lehi, and water came out of it. When Samson drank, his strength returned and he revived. So the spring was called En Hakkore, [En Hakkore means caller's spring,] and it is still there in Lehi.

Reader, you must drink of the living water that God has so freely given [the Word] that your strength returns and you become revived.

1 Samuel 30:6 KJV

> And David was distressed; for the people spake of stoning him, because the soul of all the people was grieved, every man for his sons and daughters: but David encouraged himself in his God.

2 Samuel 22:33 KJV

> God is my strength and power: and he maketh my way perfect.

2 Samuel 22:40 KJV

> For thou hast girded me with strength to battle: them that rose up against me hast thou subdued under me.

1 Chronicles 16:11

> Look to the LORD and his strength; seek his face always.

Nehemiah 8:10

> Nehemiah said, "Go and enjoy choice food and sweet drinks, and send some to those who have nothing prepared. This day is sacred to our Lord. Do not grieve, for the joy of the LORD is your strength."

Psalm 18:1-2 KJV

I will love thee, O LORD, my strength.

The LORD is my rock, and my fortress, and my deliverer; my God, my strength, in whom I will trust; my buckler, and the horn of my salvation, and my high tower.

Psalm 18:32

It is God who arms me with strength and makes my way perfect.

Psalm 22:19

But you, O LORD, be not far off; O my Strength, come quickly to help me.

Psalm 28:7

The LORD is my strength and my shield; my heart trusts in him, and I am helped. My heart leaps for joy and I will give thanks to him in song.

Psalm 28:8

The LORD is the strength of his people, a fortress of salvation for his anointed one.

Psalm 29:11

> The LORD gives strength to his people; the LORD blesses his people with peace.

Psalm 46:1 KJV

> God is our refuge and strength, a very present help in trouble.

Psalm 89:17

> For you are their glory and strength, and by your favor you exalt our horn [strong one].

Proverbs 31:25

> She is clothed with strength and dignity; she can laugh at the days to come.

Isaiah 12:2

> Surely God is my salvation; I will trust and not be afraid. The LORD, the LORD, is my strength and song; he has become my salvation.

Isaiah 33:2

> O LORD, be gracious to us; we long for you. Be our strength every morning, our salvation in time of distress.

Isaiah 40:29, 31 KJV

> He giveth power to the faint; and to them that have no might he increaseth strength.
>
> But they that wait upon the LORD shall renew their strength; they shall mount up with wings as eagles: they shall run, and not be weary; they shall walk, and not faint.

Isaiah 57:10

> You were wearied by all your ways, but you would not say, 'It is hopeless.' You found renewal of your strength, and so you did not faint.

Daniel 10:18, 19

> Again the one who looked like a man touched me and gave me strength. "Do not be afraid, O man highly esteemed," he said. "Peace! Be strong now; be strong." When he spoke to me, I was strengthened and said, "Speak, my lord, since you have given me strength."

Listen to the Lord. When He strengthens you, He will instruct you.

Philippians 4:13 KJV

> I can do all things through Christ which strenghteneth me.

1Timothy 1:12

> I thank Christ Jesus our Lord, who has given me strength, that he considered me faithful, appointing me to his service.

2 Timothy 4:17

> But the Lord stood at my side and gave me strength, so that through me the message might be fully proclaimed and all the Gentiles might hear it. And I was delivered from the lion's mouth.

Revelation 3:8

> I know your works: behold, I have set before you an open door, and no man can shut it: for thou hast a little strength, and hast kept my word, and hast not denied my name.

Work your faith. I am reminded of the words I used to hear on a radio ministry, "The Word works when you work the Word." God has given us what we need. According to 2 Corinthians 10:4 KJV, "The weapons of our warfare are not carnal, but mighty through God to the pulling down of strong holds." Our weapons are mighty <u>through God</u>

to the pulling down of strong holds. I understand this to mean through faith in God and His Word.

God's promise to me on a personal matter came from Isaiah 41:10 KJV, "Fear thou not; for I am with thee: be not dismayed; for I am thy God: I will strengthen thee; yea, I will help thee; yea I will uphold thee with the right hand of my righteousness." Now that's awesome! I believe it and I am convinced that God cares about everything that we go through.

I know just as satan desired to sift Peter as wheat, his desire is to destroy us also, but because Jesus does not have favorites, I claim the words He spoke to Peter in Luke 22:32 KJV, "But I have prayed for thee, that thy faith fail not: and when thou are converted, strengthen thy brethren." Matthew Henry's commentary defines converted in this passage as recovered. He states it this way, "When you are recovered by the grace of God, and brought to repentance, do what you can to recover others, encourage others to hope that they also shall find mercy."

I believe that God used my dear friend to help me to understand that there is healing in death. I wrote that in an earlier book entitled, Mama, I'll Be Strong. I had believed God for my mother's healing but she went on to be with the Lord. The smile on her face was evidence that she was healed. I believe that's how He chose to heal her, but as for us, let's stand on Psalm 27:13KJV: "I had fainted, unless I had believed to see the goodness of the Lord in the land of the living."

I just want to be real with you. I cannot make the decision for God. My assignment is to intercede for others. I can't heal anyone nor change the circumstances that they ask me to pray about—but God can. I know that He has healed countless people and they are able to share their testimonies. I believe He wants us to live and proclaim His goodness to our dying world. You must make your requests known then touch and agree with your prayer partners. God is faithful.

My friend told me near the end of her life that she was encouraged. She said that she was hoping for the best but she was preparing for the worst. She tried to prepare me too. She was so unselfish, always thinking of others.

Be encouraged on today. Remember, Malachi 4:2, "But unto you that fear my name shall the Sun of righteousness arise with healing in his wings; and ye shall go forth, and grow up as calves of the stall." You are healed. Have faith in God.

To God Be The Glory.

In Loving Memory of

Anne Whitehead Arrington

1944-2005